ON TRACK
READERS FOR ADULT STUDENTS

Valentina

Penny Cameron
Language & Culture Center
University of Houston

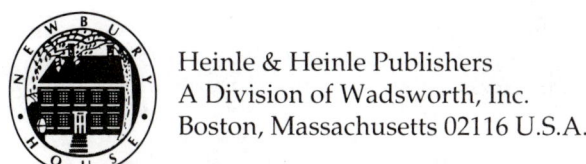

Heinle & Heinle Publishers
A Division of Wadsworth, Inc.
Boston, Massachusetts 02116 U.S.A.

Acknowledgments

The author wishes to thank the following people
for their help and advice:

Jerry Buncher

Charles Hooks

Geri Hooks

Karen Kaufman

Joseph Merlinsky

Viktor Nikolayev

Isaac Siperstein

Valentina Siperstein

Kathryn Vidal

Boris Zamsky

Publisher: Stanley J. Galek
Editorial Director: Christopher Foley
Assistant Editor: Margaret Morris
Editorial Production Manager: Elizabeth Holthaus
Manufacturing Coordinator: Jerry Christopher
Design and Composition: PC&F, Inc.
Cover Design and Illustration: Cyndy Patrick

10 9 8 7 6 5 4 3 2 1

ISBN 0-8384-2931-9

Copyright © 1992 by Heinle & Heinle Publishers

All rights reserved. No part of this publication may be reproduced or transmitted in any form or by any means, electronic, or mechanical, including photocopy, recording, or any information storage and retrieval system, without permission in writing from the publisher.

Heinle & Heinle Publishers is a division of Wadsworth, Inc.

Manufactured in the United States of America

Contents

	Introduction	iv
	To the Student	v
Chapter 1	A New Start	1
Chapter 2	Boris Finds Work	9
Chapter 3	Valentina's Jobs	17
Chapter 4	Changes	25
Chapter 5	New York, New York!	33
Chapter 6	The Creel Gallery	41
Chapter 7	The Exhibition	47
Chapter 8	Peter Malouf's Review	53
Chapter 9	Valentina and Peter	61
Chapter 10	"Where's My Chagall?"	69

Introduction

These stories are about people who are new to America. They have problems, but they overcome them. The things they learned in other places help them. And, because they're adults, they can say, "We know that!"

People learn how to do things in one place or country. When they leave, they take what they know with them. They don't forget what they already know.

Please read these stories, and think about what you already know. Use your knowledge to help you. It doesn't matter where you learned what you know!

Mrs. Lau is a grandmother. She comes to live with her son and his family. But she doesn't feel at home. Still, she wants to be with her son's children, and they're in America. Most grandmothers want to be with their grandchildren. Mrs. Lau is wise. She likes to help people, and she finds her place in America. She uses what she knows.

Julio Martinez comes from Mexico. He's learning new things all the time. When he starts to learn English, his life gets much better. He falls in love. Then things go wrong. Julio listens to another student in his class. Her experience helps him decide what to do.

Valentina Petrov comes from Russia. It's easy for her to get work, but she doesn't like her job. She loses her baby; then her marriage ends. Valentina uses what she knows from her old country. That's how she builds her new life in her new country.

Antonio Chirinos comes from Venezuela. He's a trainee in a store. He's learning about sales. Antonio already knows how to sell things. He worked in a store in his own country. A good salesperson is a good salesperson everywhere. Antonio's skill helps him to live in America. His driving experience in Caracas also helps him late one night.

To the Student

If you are reading on your own, please follow these steps:

1. Think about the title of the book or chapter. What does it mean?

2. Before you read a chapter, look at the pictures. What do you see?

3. Try to answer the **Before You Read** questions. Use your dictionary if you need help.

4. If you have the cassette tape, play it. Listen to the story. Read the story while you listen to the tape. Don't use the dictionary.

5. Play the tape and listen to the story again. Use your dictionary if you don't understand some words.

6. Play the tape and read aloud along with it. Try to copy the voice on the tape.

7. Answer the **After You Read** questions. Write notes for questions 3 and 4 if you're working alone. Write a longer answer for question 5.

Answers to the **After You Read** exercises 1 and 2 appear in the instructor's manual for this book. Ask your teacher for a copy of the manual if you don't have it. No answers are given for exercises 3, 4, and 5. For those exercises, many different answers are correct.

Chapter 1

A New Start

Before You Read

1. **Discuss this question with your classmates:**
   - Remember your first few days in the United States. How did you feel?

   Use your own words, or choose words from this list:

a little scared	confident
enthusiastic	happy
homesick	nervous

2. **Look at the picture on the facing page. Valentina Petrov and her husband, Boris, are talking to Natasha and Igor Belkin. Boris has a pipe, and Valentina is sitting next to him. Match the numbers on the picture with the words below:**

   _____ notes   _____ curtains

   _____ pipe   _____ Boris

   _____ suitcase   _____ Valentina

   _____ Natasha   _____ Igor

3. **Think about the picture and answer these questions:**
   - How old are Boris and Valentina? Are they older or younger than Igor and Natasha?
   - How does Valentina feel? Does Boris feel the same way as Valentina does?
   - What is an interview?
   - What does "training for a job" mean?

A New Start

Valentina Petrov looks around the apartment. It's bright and new. The sun shines through the window and hurts her eyes.

Natasha Belkin sees that Valentina is uncomfortable. She hurries to close the curtains.

"The sun is strong in California," Natasha says. "When we came from Russia, I was surprised. Everything was so bright."

Valentina smiles. Natasha seems to understand how she feels. And she speaks Russian, too.

Natasha says, "I was very excited to hear you were coming. You were only a little girl when I left Moscow. I remember you sat alone and drew pictures."

Valentina smiles. "I did that while I waited for Mama to finish work."

"How is your mother?" Natasha asks. "I remember her well. She was my doctor when I was a little girl. She's really good, you know."

"She's very busy," Valentina says. "Children get sick a lot."

"That's true in this country, too," Natasha adds. "I'm a nurse. I see plenty of kids." She turns to her husband. "Igor, does Boris know what we're going to do tomorrow?"

"We're talking about it now," Igor Belkin replies. "I think these young people still feel a little strange. Remember how we felt when we first arrived?"

"I remember," Natasha laughs. "Twelve years ago. It seems like yesterday." She turns to Boris and Valentina. "When we first came to America, another Russian couple helped us. They found us an apartment. Now it's our turn to help you."

Valentina smiles. "Thank you," she says. "And thank you for finding us this apartment."

Natasha and Igor smile. "It's good to have a place to come to," Natasha says. "Now, let us talk. We have some plans."

They all sit down at the table. Igor pulls out some notes.

"Tomorrow, we will take you shopping," he says. "We'll show you where to buy clothes for work.

"After that, we'll start looking for jobs. I have a list of places with me. I wrote letters to all of them about you. In fact, Boris, you can start interviews this week, if you like."

Boris looks excited. "That's very good," he says.

Valentina feels nervous and unhappy. She's not enthusiastic.

"You're lucky," Igor goes on. "There are lots of jobs for people like you. You'll both find work quite easily, I think."

Boris smiles. "Chemical engineers are useful people," he says. "Of course I can find work."

Valentina grits her teeth. The action makes her mouth hurt. "Boris is always so sure of things," she thinks. "He's so confident!" Then she makes herself smile.

Igor is speaking to Boris. "I know you both read English well," he says. "Can you speak it well, too?"

Suddenly Boris looks worried. He plays with his pipe for a while. "I don't know," he says at last. "It was difficult at the airport. Americans speak so quickly."

Natasha laughs. "They do," she agrees. "But I'm sure you'll learn. I have to tell you something, Boris. Many people in America don't like smoking. Don't take your pipe to an interview. Not even for while you are waiting."

Boris looks surprised. "Cigarettes, then?"

"No cigarettes, either," Igor says firmly. "Americans don't smoke very much. They say it's unhealthy. Leave your cigarettes at home."

Igor turns to Valentina. "You have a good education, too," he says. "Businesses need people like you to do technical drawing. In Moscow you worked as a draftsperson, didn't you?"

"Yes, I did, for five years," Valentina says. "But I want to do something else in America."

"What do you want to do?" Natasha asks.

"I really like to draw and paint," Valentina says. "I'd like to work with art."

"That's difficult," Natasha replies. "It's hard to get those jobs. Do you have any special education in art?"

"No," Valentina replies, "only my training in industrial design."

"Perhaps you can work with art later," Igor says. "Right now, I think you should work as a draftsperson. There are more jobs for draftspersons than for artists."

Valentina sinks back in her chair. She's no longer interested in working. Natasha pats her arm. "What is it?" she asks.

"I don't know," Valentina replies. "I feel strange. One day we're in Moscow, and now ..." She doesn't finish her sentence. "I miss my mother, I guess," Valentina says. "I'm afraid that I'll never see her again."

Natasha puts her hand on Valentina's arm. "Don't say that," she says. "Strange things can happen. Maybe one day your mother will visit you here in America."

Valentina doesn't believe that her mother will ever come to the United States. She smiles politely at Natasha.

Boris puts his arm around his wife. "Don't worry about your mother now," he says. "We're here to make a new start, remember?"

Valentina tries to smile again, but she can't.

Natasha and Igor tell Boris what to do the next day. Valentina sits and listens quietly. She's glad that Natasha and Igor are there to help.

At last the Belkins leave. Boris says good-bye at the door. Then he comes back to Valentina.

They look at each other. "You're right, Boris," Valentina says. "This is the beginning of a new part of our lives. I won't look back. Well, not too much!"

After You Read

1. Circle the best word to complete each sentence.

Valentina and Boris Petrov are in San Francisco. They have come from (1) (*New York Moscow California*). Another Russian couple, Igor and Natasha, are helping the Petrovs to make (2) (*plans notes curtains*). Boris is very excited about a new (3) (*pipe apartment job*). Boris is sure that he will get work because he's a (4) (*doctor chemical engineer draftsperson*). Valentina wants a job in (5) (*art industrial design nursing*). She wishes she could see her (6) (*children mother little girl*).

Complete each sentence with one of the words below:

enthusiastic	plans
plays with	politely
surprised	training
uncomfortable	worried

1. Boris is **worried** because he can't understand spoken English well.

2. Boris picks up his pipe and _____ it.

3. Valentina smiled _____ at Natasha because she wanted to make Natasha happy. Valentina was not happy herself.

4. When people make _____ they decide what they will do in the future.

5. The sun _____ Valentina because she wasn't expecting it to be so bright.

A NEW START   5

6. Boris is _____ about looking for a job, but Valentina isn't.

7. When you have _____ in something, you know how to do it.

8. If something hurts you, but not badly, you feel _____ .

3. **Our bodies show how we feel.**

   "Valentina grits her teeth. The action makes her mouth hurt."

   Show the class, draw a picture, or write a description below:
   - What happens when you "grit your teeth?" Why do you do it?

   "Then she makes herself smile."
   - How do you make yourself smile? Are you really happy when you do it?

   "Valentina sinks back in her chair."
   - What does "sink back" mean? How do you feel when you sit like that?

4. **Discuss the questions below with your classmates. Make notes on what you decide.**
   - What kinds of things are important to Boris and to Valentina?
   - Are the same things important to each of them? How do you know?

5. **Pretend you are Igor Belkin. You're talking with your wife, Natasha, on the way home. What do you think of Boris and Valentina? Role-play the situation with a**

classmate. One student can be Igor, and another student can be Natasha.

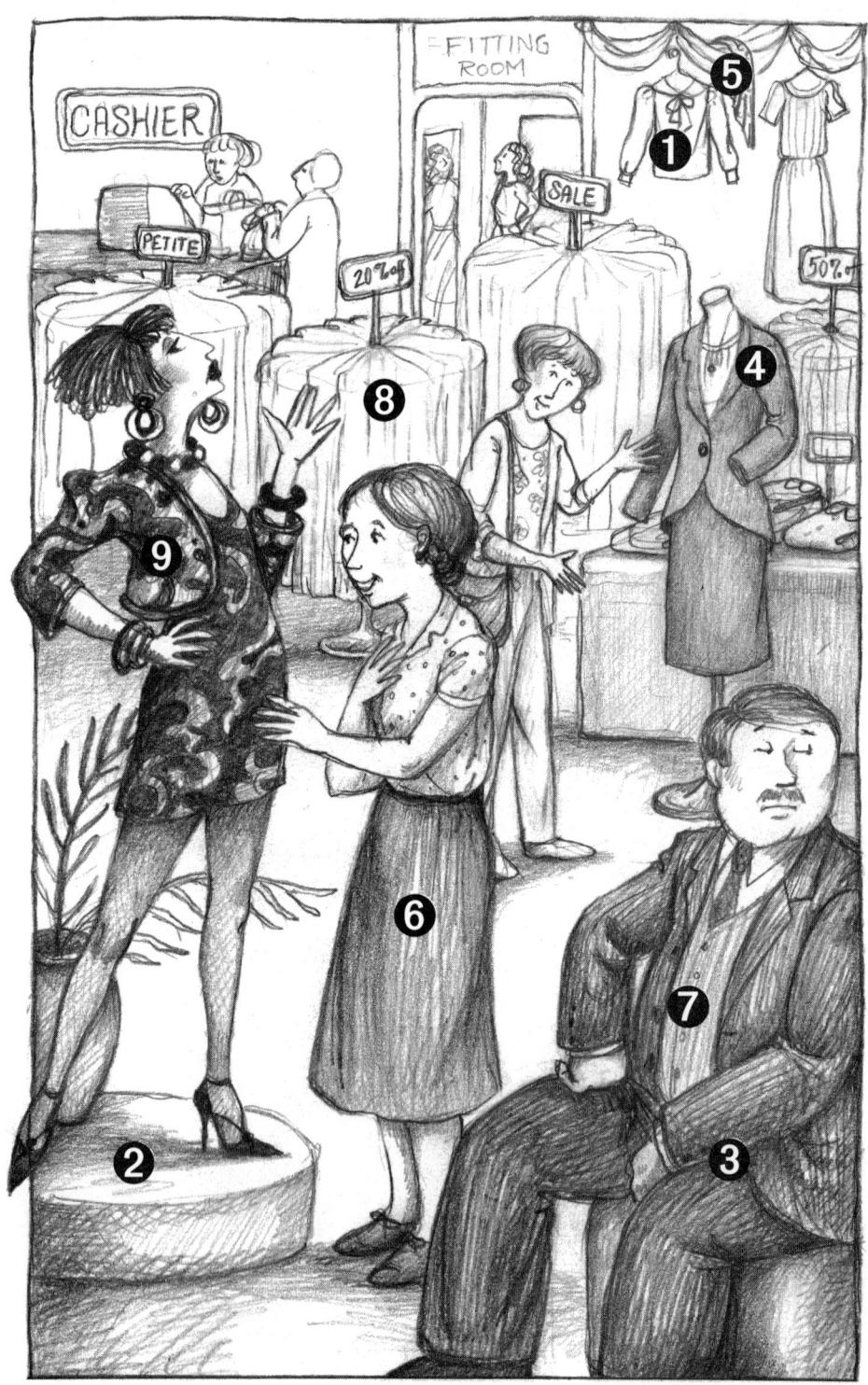

Chapter 2

Boris Finds Work

Before You Read

1. Discuss these questions with your classmates:
   - What kind of clothes do you wear to an interview?

   Use your own words, or choose words from the list:

bright colors	businesslike
conservative	plain
shorts	short skirt
simple	

   - Why do you choose special clothes for an interview?

2. Look at the picture on page 8. Valentina is looking at a store mannequin. Match the numbers on the picture with the words and phrases below:

   _____ store mannequin   _____ skirt

   _____ jacket   _____ racks of clothes

   _____ gray suit   _____ blouse

   _____ woman's business suit   _____ scarf

   _____ buttons

3. Think about the picture and answer these questions:
   - How does Boris feel?
   - How does Valentina feel?

Use your own words, or choose words from this list:

amazed   bored   excited
nervous   patient

- What clothes do you think Valentina likes?

4. **Look at the picture above. Jane O'Brien is directing Igor and Boris to a small table in the corner of her office.**

- What is Jane O'Brien's job?

Boris Finds Work

Natasha Belkin arrives the next day to take the Petrovs shopping.

First they look for clothes for Boris. They visit the men's department of a large store. Boris tries on a dark gray wool suit. It looks good.

Natasha chooses another suit. It's not so dark.

"Try this one, too," she says. "I think you'll like it."

Boris likes the suit he's wearing. He doesn't want to try on any more suits.

"I will keep this one," he says. "Thank you."

Natasha finds some shirts and ties. Boris tries them on with the suit. He looks great! He doesn't want to take off his new clothes.

They pay for the new clothes and put the old ones in a bag. Then they go to the women's department.

Valentina is amazed. There are racks and racks of clothes! The colors are beautiful. Valentina goes from rack to rack, looking at every item. Boris finds a chair and sits down. He knows he's going to wait a long time.

Valentina looks closely at a dress on a store mannequin. The dress has a short skirt and a jacket. The fabric is soft, with a rich design.

Valentina touches the jacket gently. "It's so beautiful," she says.

"It is," Natasha agrees. "But it's not what we want. You need a nice suit to wear to your interviews. A dark blue, perhaps, or a gray …"

Valentina's face falls. Then she sees a bright yellow dress, with big buttons down the front. A black and orange scarf is tied at the neck.

"What about this?" she asks hopefully.

"It's very pretty, but it's not right for an interview," Natasha says firmly. "We have to find a quiet, plain suit." She picks out a gray suit with a light-colored blouse.

"But that looks just like Boris's suit with a skirt," Valentina cries. She looks around the store. There are so many clothes, so many choices.

At last Valentina and Natasha agree on a dark blue suit with a light blue blouse. They buy the clothes, find Boris, then leave the store.

Natasha takes them to a coffee shop for lunch. She leaves the table to make a phone call.

Valentina looks around. Some of the women are wearing dark suits. Others are wearing bright clothes and jewelry.

Natasha returns to the table. "I just spoke to Igor," she says. "You have an interview with Globe Chemicals at 3:00 P.M., Boris. Do you think you are ready?"

Boris looks down at his new suit and tie. "Of course I am ready," he replies, smiling.

After lunch, they find their way to the business part of town. It's almost time for Boris's interview.

Natasha leads them into the lobby of a large building. Igor is there waiting for them.

"You're right on time," Igor says. "That's good, Boris, we're going to see Ms. O'Brien. She's the head of personnel for Globe Chemicals. I wrote to her about you. She knows a lot about your work." Igor sounds excited. "I'll tell you about the job. This is a good company."

Valentina kisses Boris. He smiles nervously, then walks to the elevator with Igor. Igor is talking quickly. Valentina and Natasha leave the building.

Igor and Boris wait in a little room outside Ms. O'Brien's office. After five minutes, a door opens. "Please come in," a woman says. She directs them to a small table in the corner of the room. An Asian man is sitting at the table.

"I'm Jane O'Brien," the woman says. "I'm glad you could come, too, Mr. Belkin. You can explain things to Mr. Petrov."

Igor smiles. "Thank you for inviting me," he says.

"I've asked Dr. Tom Chang to join us," Ms. O'Brien says. "He's our vice president for research. Dr. Chang's very interested in your work, Mr. Petrov."

Dr. Chang and Boris talk for a while. Igor and Ms. O'Brien sit and listen.

It's easy for Boris to talk to Dr. Chang. They both know a lot about their subject, chemistry. It's not so easy for Boris to talk to Ms. O'Brien.

After about half an hour, Jane O'Brien interrupts the two men. "I'd like to talk to Dr. Chang for a moment. Would you two gentlemen please wait outside?"

Igor and Boris return to the waiting room and sit down. Boris is nervous. He wishes he could smoke. He looks around and sees a sign. It reads, "Thank you for not smoking."

"I cannot smoke here?" he asks Igor, pointing to the sign.

"That's right, Boris. You can't," Igor replies. "The sign is a polite way to tell you."

The door to Ms. O'Brien's office opens.

"Please come back in," the personnel director says. She leads them back into the room and waits for them to sit down. "I'm concerned about your English, Mr. Petrov. However, Dr. Chang says that you speak enough English to work in his laboratory. I hope that you will be able to speak more easily soon."

She pauses, then says, "We have a position for you, Mr. Petrov. Dr. Chang would like you to work in his research laboratory. Will you accept?"

Boris turns to Igor. He doesn't know what to say.

"Let's talk about the salary and conditions," Igor says. "How much will you pay? What will his job responsibilities be?"

— • — • —

That night Boris, Valentina, Igor, and Natasha eat a big meal to celebrate. Boris has a job! After just one interview, too!

Boris is very happy. Valentina hopes that she'll be lucky, too. But she's not looking forward to doing technical drawings.

After You Read

1. **Write *T* if the statement is true and *F* if it's false. If the statement is false, write the true statement below it.**

   __F__ 1. Boris is excited about buying clothes.
   Boris is not very interested in buying clothes.

   ____ 2. Valentina likes bright colors and designs.

   ____ 3. A dark suit is best for an interview.

   ____ 4. Igor takes Boris to his interview.

   ____ 5. Boris understands Dr. Chang because Dr. Chang speaks Russian.

   ____ 6. Boris doesn't get a job.

2. **Match the words in column A with their meaning in column B.**

A	B
1. lobby	a. money received for a job
2. amazed	b. downstairs part of a building
3. directs	c. comes in between, stops
4. design	d. very surprised
5. interrupts	e. points to
6. firmly	f. arrangement of shapes
7. salary	g. have a party for a special reason
8. celebrate	h. strongly

3. **Read quickly through Chapter 2 again to find the answer to the following question. Before you begin, look at your watch. See how long it takes you to find the answer. Write your answer and your time below.**

   • What is the name of the company Boris will work for?

   Answer: _____

   Time: _____

4. **Write answers to the following questions:**
   - What does "bored" mean? Where in Chapter 2 is someone bored?

   _____

   _____

   _____

   - How do people sit when they're bored?

   Show the class, write a description, or draw a picture on a piece of paper.

5. **Discuss the following questions with your classmates:**
   - Will Boris like working at Globe Chemicals? Why or why not?
   - How does Valentina feel about her husband's new job?

6. **Do people usually find work easily? Did you ever find a job as quickly as Boris did? Tell the class. OR: Write about your own situation.**

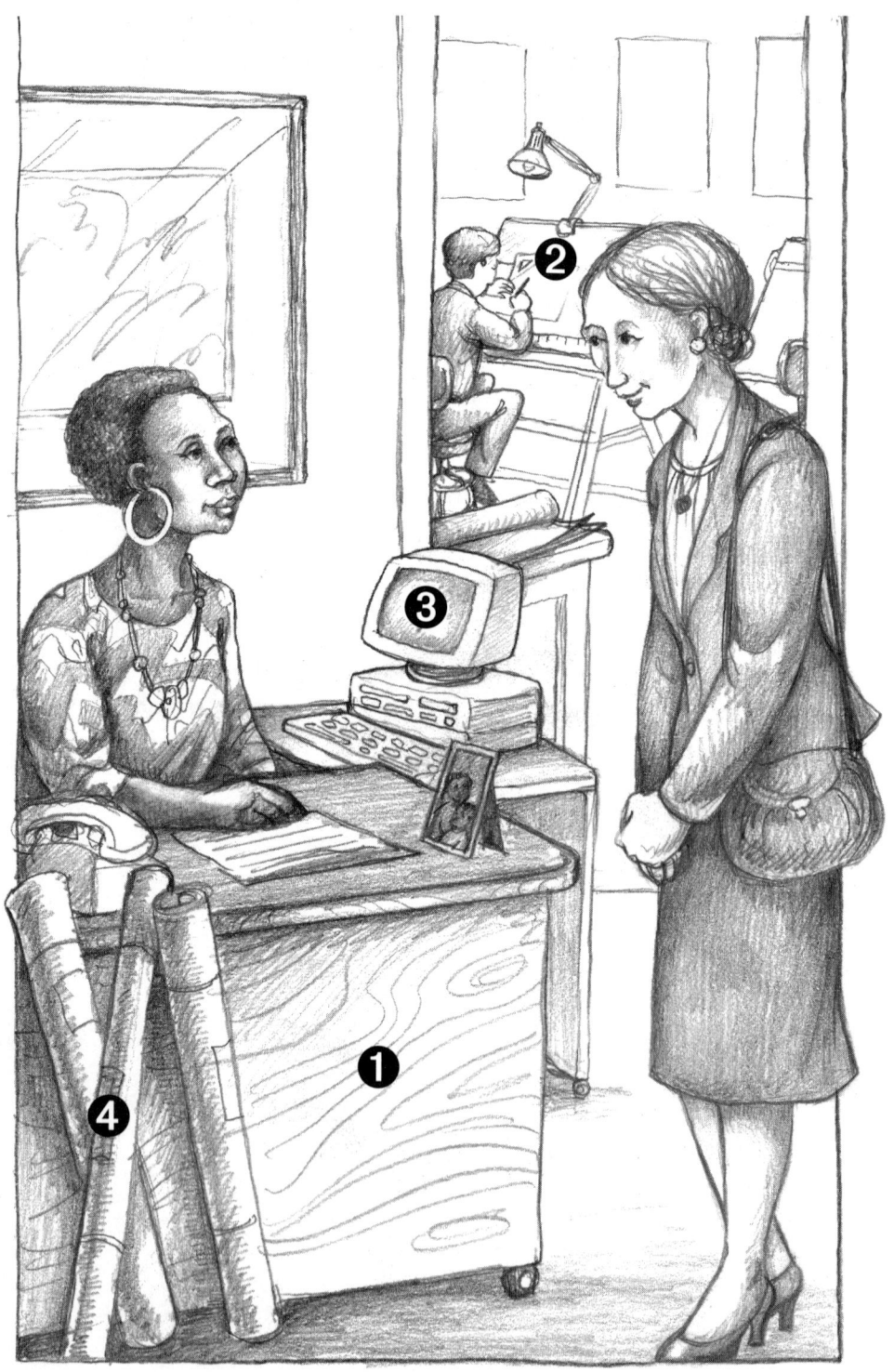

VALENTINA

Chapter 3

Valentina's Jobs

Before You Read

1. Discuss this question with your classmates:
   - What jobs do you think Valentina has?

2. Look at the picture on page 16. Valentina is talking to the receptionist. Match the numbers on the picture with the words and phrases below.

   _____ computer   _____ drawing board

   _____ desk   _____ building plans

3. Think about the picture and answer these questions:
   - What is Valentina wearing? Why is she dressed like that?
   - Where is Valentina? Why is she there?

4. Look at the picture on page 18. Valentina is in the kitchen of her apartment. Match the numbers on the picture with the words below.

   _____ dishes   _____ sink   _____ cupboard

   _____ coffee mug _____ dishwasher

5. Think about the picture and answer these questions:
   - How does Valentina feel? Why?
   - What is Boris doing? How does he feel?

   Use your own words, or choose words from this list:

   | angry | calm | frustrated |
   | irritable | tired | unworried |

17

Valentina's Jobs

Four weeks have passed. Boris is already working at his new job. Valentina is going to interviews. Today she has another interview appointment. Natasha is driving her there.

"Try to smile more," Natasha tells Valentina. "Make them think that you really want the job."

"Can you come with me?" Valentina asks.

"I'm sorry," Natasha replies, "I must go to the hospital. You'll have to go by yourself."

Valentina feels nervous. "What if I can't speak?" she asks. "What if I don't understand?"

"What did they tell you in your English class?" Natasha asks.

"The teacher said to smile," Valentina replies, smiling. "Then I say, 'Please repeat that.'"

"See?" Natasha responds. "Just as I said. Look as though the job is important to you." She stops the car in front of a building. "Here we are," she says. "Jump out quickly. I'll call you later."

Natasha drives away, and Valentina enters the building slowly. She looks at the directory board and finds the right office. The receptionist greets her there.

"Are you Ms. Petrov?" she asks.

Valentina smiles. "Yes, I am," she replies.

"Mr. Antonelli is expecting you," the receptionist says. "Will you come with me, please?"

Valentina follows the receptionist into an office. Mr. Antonelli is standing near the window. He turns around and smiles at Valentina.

He offers her a chair, and they both sit down.

"Let me tell you about the job," he says, after introducing himself. "This is a very small company. I have two draftspersons. I need one more.

"Because our company is small, there are many different things to do."

Valentina finds herself getting interested. A job with different things to do? That's good. She hates doing the same thing over and over. She asks Mr. Antonelli some questions. Their conversation is slow, but she can make him understand.

After talking some more, Mr. Antonelli offers Valentina the job. The pay is not very good, but she accepts. She's tired of going to interviews.

Valentina leaves the office feeling happy.

When she gets home, Boris is already there. The room is full of smoke from his pipe. A coffee mug is next to his chair. The coffee is cold.

At first, Boris doesn't look up when Valentina enters. Then he puts his book down and asks, "What happened?"

"I got the job," Valentina says.

"That's great," Boris says. "When do you start?"

"On Monday," Valentina says. "That's three days from now. Let's invite Igor and Natasha for a party. I want to celebrate."

Boris looks uneasy. "Why don't we wait a few days? I need to read this book," he says. "It has a lot of important information for my research."

"All right," Valentina says, but she feels angry. They celebrated for his job. Why not for hers? Besides, Boris needs a break. He's always working. He works at home, in the office ... Why, he reads chemical engineering books even in bed!

—·—·—

A few weeks later, Valentina is at her job. It's not very interesting. She looks at her watch. Should she go to lunch early? She decides to leave the office.

It's a lovely day. The sun is shining. The air feels cool and good. Valentina walks to a sandwich shop and buys her lunch. Then she sits down at an outdoor table.

She'd like to visit an art gallery, but there isn't one nearby. She misses being near pictures. "I must find out about galleries," she thinks. Her eyes feel very heavy. She folds her arms on the table and rests her head on top. In a few minutes, she's asleep.

Fifteen minutes later, Valentina wakes up. It's already past her lunch hour! She hurries back to the office. Mr. Antonelli is waiting for her.

"I need to speak to you, Valentina," he says. They go into his office.

"This can't go on," Mr. Antonelli says, "Your English is much better, but now there's another problem. You have to understand this, Valentina. You need to be here when the work comes in. The other draftspersons can't do their work and yours, too. You have to do your share. If you don't work harder, I'm afraid you'll lose your job."

"I'm sorry," Valentina says. She really is. She returns to her desk. The other people look at her angrily.

Valentina works hard all afternoon, then hurries home. Boris is there in his usual cloud of smoke. It makes her sick. She goes into the kitchen. The breakfast dishes are still in the sink.

"It's not hard to put things in a dishwasher," she calls to Boris angrily. "You can help more around the house. I go to work, too. I don't need two jobs, one at work, one at home."

She goes to the bedroom. The bed is unmade. She lies down on it anyway.

That night Valentina calls Natasha. She tells her how she feels. Natasha listens, then asks, "How do you feel in the mornings?"

"I don't know, a little strange, I guess," Valentina replies. "Sometimes I feel sick until I eat." She pauses and asks nervously, "Natasha, do you think I might be pregnant?"

"Hmm. A little sick in the morning, tired during the day, irritable ... Yes, Valentina, it's possible. Maybe you're going to have a baby!"

• •
After You Read

1. **Write Y (yes), N (no), or M (maybe) before these statements. If you write M, explain your answer to the class.**

    __Y__ 1. Valentina likes her job, but she doesn't love it.

    _____ 2. Boris loves housework.

___ 3. Boris enjoys his job.

___ 4. Boris will change jobs very soon.

___ 5. Boris will be pleased that Valentina is pregnant.

___ 6. Valentina and Boris will be good parents.

2. **Find words in Chapter 3 to complete the sentences below:**

    1. Valentina goes to her interview at a special time. She has an **appointment**.

    2. A _____ lists the names and office numbers of people in the building.

    3. The person who greets Valentina when she gets to the office is the _____.

    4. People who do technical drawings are called _____.

    5. Works of art are often hung in a _____.

    6. Mr. Antonelli says that Valentina must do her _____ of the work in the office.

    7. A _____ is a machine that washes dishes.

    8. When a woman is going to have a baby, she's _____.

3. **Discuss the questions below with your classmates. Make notes on what you decide.**
    - What kind of person is Boris? Is he a good husband?
    - Will Boris be a good father? Why or why not?

4. **Do you think Boris and Valentina will be good parents? How do you know? Write your reasons below.**

_____

_____

_____

5. **Talk or write about your answer to the following question:**
   - What ideas or advice would you give to Boris and Valentina?

Chapter 4

Changes

Before You Read

1. **Discuss these questions with your classmates:**
   - Have you ever had a big change in your life? How did you feel?

   Use your own words, or choose words from this list:

excited	nervous
very frightened	happy
sad	worried

2. **Look at the picture on page 24. Boris is hugging Valentina. Think about the picture and answer these questions:**
   - How does Boris feel?
   - Why does he feel that way?

   Use your own words, or choose words from this list:

happy	pleased
proud	tender

3. **Look at the picture on page 26. Valentina is hiding near the elevators in an office building. Match the numbers on the picture with the words below:**

   _____ elevators   _____ lobby

   _____ entrance   _____ exit

   - How does Valentina feel? Why do you think so?

Changes

Valentina visits a doctor and learns that she is pregnant. She writes to her mother right away. But she waits a few days before telling Boris the news. She wants it to be her secret. She likes to think of the baby growing inside her.

When she does tell Boris, he is delighted. "It will be a lovely baby," he says. "Our little 'Made in America' baby. I'm so proud and happy."

He gives Valentina a gentle hug.

Valentina laughs. "I won't break," she says. "But I will need your help, Boris. I cannot do all the work around here."

Boris looks worried. "I have a lot to read for my job," he says. "So much is happening at work. Dr. Chang is a great chemist. We're doing some exciting experiments. If I do well, it's good for you, and the baby, too."

"That's true," Valentina says. "But you can still help. It's not good for the baby if I get too tired."

The next six weeks pass quietly. Valentina is content. She takes good care of herself. She sees her doctor and eats well. Valentina's mother writes often. Her letters are always full of good advice.

Everyone is excited. Natasha telephones every few days to see how Valentina feels.

Valentina is careful to be on time at work. Mr. Antonelli does not have to speak to her again. She feels happy, and she works hard. The job doesn't seem so boring now. And she's beginning to speak English very well. She's glad she had to learn English at school in Moscow. It seemed silly when she was in Russia. But it helps now that she is in America.

One day after work Valentina finds a letter in her mailbox. It's from New York. She opens it and reads:

> 340 Amsterdam Avenue, #508
> New York, New York 10024
>
> Monday

Dear Valentina,

Do you remember me? We were neighbors in Moscow. We used to play together after school. Well, I live in New York now. My mother heard that you were in America. She went to see your mother and asked for your address. So now I am writing to you. Can you come and visit me in New York? There's an extra bed in my apartment. The place is very small, but there's always room for an old friend.

More news! I'm getting married soon—to an American. His name is Rick Oller. I met him at work. I'm very happy, but I miss my old friends.

My telephone number is (212) 721-3245. Call me if you can.

With love,
Larisa

Valentina is glad to hear from Larisa. "It would be nice to see her again," Valentina thinks. She decides to call. She dials the number, but there's no answer. Valentina looks at her watch. Of course! It's 6:00 P.M. in California, and 9:00 P.M. in New York. Larisa must be out.

Valentina hangs up the telephone. Suddenly, she feels a strong strange pain. Something is terribly wrong.

"The baby!" Valentina thinks. She walks slowly to her bed and lies down. The pain is very strong.

She lies very still and waits for the pain to stop. But it doesn't stop. It starts, then stops, then starts again. Valentina is very frightened.

Boris arrives home. Valentina hears him at the front door. "Boris," Valentina cries out. "Come quickly!" Her voice is high with fear.

Boris rushes to the bedroom. He sees the terror on his wife's face. He reaches for the phone and calls the doctor.

— . — . —

Three hours later, Boris returns from the hospital, alone. Valentina will spend the night there. There will be no baby.

— . — . —

Valentina feels sad and empty. The doctor says she can have another baby. But she doesn't want another one. She wants the baby she and Boris lost. They had dreams for their little 'Made in America' baby …

Boris is very kind to Valentina. He helps her around the house. But for Valentina it's like living with a stranger.

Valentina's mother writes often. "Do something good for yourself," she says. "Try to play a little. Do the things you like to do. Go to a gallery, listen to some music."

After a week, Valentina goes back to work. Mr. Antonelli and her colleagues are very understanding. Life goes on as before, but nothing seems the same.

Six weeks after losing the baby, Valentina has a day off from work. She decides to visit an art gallery. There's one near Boris's office. Valentina decides to surprise Boris at lunchtime. Maybe they can eat together.

She enters the lobby of Boris's building from the west side. She walks toward the elevators in the center of the building. After pushing the button, she turns around.

Across the lobby, just outside the building, she sees Boris. He's laughing. And he's arm in arm with a woman.

Valentina cannot see the woman's face. Boris and the woman turn and hurry down the steps, still laughing and talking.

Valentina steps back from the elevator. Her heart is pounding. She cannot breathe.

She makes herself leave the building and return home.

Back in the apartment, Valentina finds a chair and sits down. For a long time she sits and thinks about her life in America. First she lost her baby. Now, maybe, she has lost Boris, too. It is all very sad.

But it's also strange. When she thinks about it, she doesn't really care about losing Boris. It was a shock to see him with another woman. But at the same time, it doesn't hurt too much. Not like the baby.

Later in the afternoon, Boris comes home. Valentina has a meal ready.

"Who did you have lunch with?" she asks.

"Someone from work," Boris replies. "As usual. Why do you ask?"

Valentina feels a little sick. "I went to your office," she says calmly. "I thought we could have lunch together. I saw you with a woman."

Boris stops eating. "You must mean Marianna," he says. "An excellent chemist! She's doing wonderful work." The words sound full of truth, but Boris's face is turning red. He looks away quickly.

Valentina gets up and leaves the room. She lies down on the bed and cries. Boris stays at the table. After a while, he gets up. Valentina hears him moving in the kitchen. Then, she smells the smoke of his pipe.

— · — · —

Over the next few days, Valentina thinks hard. Finally, she makes a decision. She knows what she will do.

Valentina calls Larisa in New York. The following day, she resigns from her job. She will leave her work in two weeks.

Mr. Antonelli is sorry to see Valentina leave. Valentina doesn't really feel anything.

The last two weeks in California are sad for Valentina. She and Boris talk, but things are not the same. They feel differently about each other. Now the marriage and the baby are both dead.

Valentina looks forward to a change, to New York, to a new life. She remembers her words the first day in the apartment, "I won't look back."

• •

After You Read

1. **Number these sentences in the correct order (1–6):**

   _____ Valentina resigns from her job.

__1__ Valentina tells Boris about the baby.

____ Valentina sees Boris with another woman.

____ Valentina has a letter from her friend in New York.

____ Valentina loses her baby.

____ Valentina decides to visit Larisa in New York.

2. **These words are from Chapter 4. Choose five of them, and write sentences of your own.**

advice	calmly	change
delighted	empty	frightened
pain	resigns	secret
suddenly		

   1. _____
   2. _____
   3. _____
   4. _____
   5. _____

3. **What were Valentina's feelings when she saw Boris and Marianna? How do people stand or move when they are shocked? Afraid? Show or tell the class.**

4. **Imagine you are Valentina. Write a letter to your mother, and tell her what happened.**

5. **Discuss the questions below with your classmates. Make notes on what you decide and report your answers to the class.**
   - What's going to happen? Will Boris and Valentina get back together again? Is their marriage really over?

VALENTINA

Chapter 5

New York, New York!

Before You Read

1. **Discuss this question with your classmates:**
   - What do you know about New York?

   Use your own words, or choose words from this list:

big	busy	dangerous
exciting	expensive	fast
noisy		

2. **Look at the picture on page 32. Larisa and Valentina are meeting at Grand Central Station. Match the numbers on the picture with the words and phrases below:**

   _____ luggage   _____ curly hair

   _____ checked scarf

3. **Think about the picture and answer this question:**
   - How do Valentina and Larisa feel?

4. **Look at the picture on page 34. Wayne Briggs is talking to Valentina in his office. Match the numbers on the picture with the words below:**

   _____ filing cabinets   _____ pencils

   _____ pens

5. **Think about the picture and answer this question:**
   - What kind of person is Wayne Briggs?

33

Use your own words, or choose words from this list:

businesslike concerned
very neat and organized worried

34 VALENTINA

New York, New York!

Valentina takes a train across the United States to New York. The trip is long, but she enjoys it. Her life is changing. She needs time to think. She feels free—free to enjoy the space, free to be herself.

She also enjoys talking to the people on the train. She talks to everyone in English. Her English is much better now. She learns a lot about how Americans think. At last the train arrives at New York's Grand Central Station.

Larisa is waiting for Valentina. She's waving a yellow and black checked scarf.

Valentina recognizes Larisa right away. She hasn't changed much at all. Her face is still round, and her hair very curly. The hair is hard to control, just as it always was.

The two women embrace when they meet. Then they laugh. "It's so good to see someone from the past," Larisa says. "Valentina, you look wonderful!"

"Thank you, Larisa. You look great, too," Valentina replies.

The two women get Valentina's luggage and leave the station. Valentina looks around at all the movement in New York. "This is a new beginning," she thinks.

They take a taxi to Larisa's apartment. It's very small, just as Larisa said. They sit and talk for a while about the past, about Moscow, their families. Finally, they talk about the present and their futures. Valentina tells Larisa about the baby and about Boris. Larisa listens quietly.

"How long can you stay?" Larisa asks when Valentina finishes her story.

"I'd like to get to know the city," Valentina says. "And I must find a job."

She pauses. "May I stay until I get settled?" she asks cautiously.

"Of course," Larisa says without hesitation. "And you must meet my fiancé."

That night Rick Oller comes for dinner. Valentina likes him. "He and Larisa will be good together," she thinks. Then, for a moment, she feels sad. She and Boris were in love once, too ... It seems a long time ago.

For the next few days, Valentina walks around New York. She discovers the Metropolitan Museum of Art. She spends hours in the Cloisters, looking at old paintings. She is happy in a different way now. She feels sure that something good will happen. She just has to wait.

Valentina enjoys the city. She walks around the Lower West Side. She looks at the small art galleries there. She wishes she could afford to buy a painting or two.

She writes a letter to her mother.

> 340 Amsterdam Ave.
> Tuesday

Dear Mama,

I am in New York now, visiting Larisa.

I miss Boris, but every day I miss him less. Our marriage is all over. I left him because I was ready to go, and I am happy.

Mama, New York is an exciting city! I wish I could show it to you!

Stay well.

> I love you,
> *Valentina*

A few days later, Valentina sees a sign in the window of a gallery. It reads, "We need a person who understands Russian and art. Please apply within."

Valentina steps into the gallery. The people inside are well dressed. She looks down at her own clothes: jeans and sneakers. She can't go in. This is the time for her dark blue interview suit.

Valentina rushes back to the apartment and changes her

clothes. She puts on her interview suit and hurries back to the gallery.

As she stands outside the gallery door, she feels nervous. Then she draws a deep breath and steps inside.

A short, square-looking man approaches her.

"What may I show you?" he asks.

"I saw the sign in your window," Valentina says. "My name is Valentina Petrov. I speak Russian, and I know about art." She puts out her hand. The man shakes it and looks at her closely.

"Come with me," he says.

They walk to the back of the showroom and into a small office. Several filing cabinets line the walls. A computer sits on the desk. Everything is very neat and organized. The pens and pencils lie in straight rows on the desk.

The man offers Valentina a chair. She sits down.

"My name is Wayne Briggs," he says. "I'm the business manager for this gallery. Tell me about yourself, Ms. Petrov."

Valentina's hands feel cold. She really wants to say the right thing.

"You need somebody who understands Russian," she begins. "Russian is my first language."

"I guessed that," Wayne Briggs replies.

"I grew up in Moscow," Valentina says. "I spent a lot of time in the Tretyakov Gallery. I know a lot about Russian art."

"I know the Tretyakov. It's a great gallery," Wayne Briggs says. "Did you study art at school or university?"

"Neither one," Valentina replies. "But, I went to lectures at the gallery as often as possible. I'm a trained draftsperson. I understand space very well. I can tell you about paintings. I know why a picture is made the way it is."

Wayne leans back in his chair. He looks interested. He seems to be thinking.

"Ms. Petrov," he says, "Let me tell you a little about this gallery."

After You Read

1. Circle the best word to complete each sentence.

Valentina travels by train to (1) (*The Lower West Side   New York   the Tretykov Gallery*). She arrives at (2) (*Grand Central Station   The Metropolitan Museum of Art   The Cloisters*). Her friend (3) (*Larisa   Rick Oller   Boris*) is waiting for her. Larisa and Valentina are (4) (*sad   sure   happy*) to see each other. Valentina meets Larisa's (5) (*friend   fiancé   manager*), Rick Oller.

Valentina (6) (*hates   likes   doesn't care about*) New York. She applies for a job at (7) (*a library   an art gallery   a school*).

2. Circle the phrases (a, b, or c) closest in meaning to the underlined phrases below:

1. The two women <u>embrace</u> when they meet.

    a. cry

    (b.) put their arms around each other

    c. say hello

2. "Of course," Larisa says <u>without hesitation</u>.

    a. right away

    b. after a moment

    c. without caring

3. "<u>Neither one</u>," Valentina replies.

    a. not one or the other

    b. both

    c. one or the other

38   VALENTINA

4. "I went to <u>lectures</u> at the gallery as often as possible."

   a. readings

   b. talks

   c. parties

3. **Why was Larisa glad to see Valentina? Write your reasons on a piece of paper. Then compare your notes with your classmates'.**

4. **Pretend you are Valentina's mother. Tell your friends (the class) about Valentina's life in America. Look back at Chapters 1–4 if you want to, and make any notes below.**

5. **What do people do who work in art galleries? Tell the class, or write your ideas below.**

40 VALENTINA

Chapter 6

The Creel Gallery

Before You Read

1. **Discuss these questions with your classmates:**
   - What can Valentina do for the art gallery? How many people in New York know about Russian art? How many people in New York speak Russian?
   - What is an exhibition of paintings?
   - What happens when somebody has a stroke?

2. **Look at the picture on page 40. Valentina is talking to Larisa. Match the numbers on the pictures with the words below:**

   _____ sofa   _____ cushion   _____ curtains

3. **Think about the picture and answer these questions:**
   - How does Larisa feel?
   - What's the trouble?
   - How can Valentina help Larisa? Is it good to be with a friend when you're upset?

The Creel Gallery

Wayne Briggs begins telling his story.

"The Creel Gallery belongs to William Creel. He opened the gallery ten years ago. He knows quite a lot about art.

"I joined Mr. Creel eight years ago. The business was growing then. Mr. Creel wanted somebody to take care of the books, the sales, you know. As I told you, I'm the business manager. I also sell paintings to the customers.

"Since then, we've done very well. William Creel leaves all money matters to me. Recently, we decided we were ready to expand.

"William heard about an exhibition of Russian paintings. It's just right for this gallery. It's the right size. It has the right kind of works for our customers.

"William is very fond of Russian art. He knows a lot about it. He can speak and read Russian. He said the exhibition would be a great chance for us.

"Anyway, we borrowed a lot of money to get this exhibition. A lot.

"Everything was going well. The paintings arrived on time. They're here in New York. We will hang them this week, on Wednesday and Thursday." Mr. Briggs pauses.

Valentina looks at him. "What's the problem?" she wonders.

"The gallery opens at 2:00 P.M. on Sundays. Last Sunday morning Mr. Creel came here alone. I came to work at 1:30 P.M. and found him. He was lying on the floor."

Valentina's eyes open wide in surprise.

Wayne Briggs pauses again, swallows hard, then goes on. "The doctors say he had a stroke. Anyway, I called an ambulance, and it took him to a hospital.

"William won't be able to work for a long time, the doctor says. And this new exhibition is opening! I know very little about the pictures. Most of the notes are written in Russian. I can't read them. So you can see why I need a Russian art expert."

Valentina smiles. "I'm not a Russian art expert," she says, "but I know something about Russian art. I can help you with the art notes. And I'd really like to work in your gallery."

Wayne Briggs leans back in his chair again. He looks doubtful.

"When does your exhibition open?" Valentina asks.

"We have the opening party on Friday. Today is Tuesday," Wayne says. He rises from his chair. "Ms. Petrov, I will offer you the job. But I must tell you, it will probably be for a short time only.

I need your help with this exhibition. After that, I cannot promise you a job. I don't know what will happen."

Valentina jumps out of her chair. She wants to kiss this man! Wayne Briggs looks nervous.

"Thank you, Mr. Briggs," Valentina says politely. "I want to work here very much." She sits down again. "Now, can we talk about money?"

— · — · —

That night Valentina and Larisa are sitting on the sofa in the living room. Larisa is leaning back on the cushions. She feels tired.

Valentina tells Larisa about the job. "Do you want me to find another apartment?" Valentina asks.

Larisa looks worried. "Actually, no," she says. "I'd like it if you stayed here. Things are changing at work. I might have to go to Boston. My boss wants me to. Rick is trying to get a transfer also. I just don't know what's going to happen." Larisa looks miserable.

Valentina puts her arm around her friend. "But that's good news, isn't it?" she asks gently.

"I guess it is and it isn't," Larisa replies. "Rick doesn't like the idea. He doesn't like following me. We always thought *he* would go first, and I would follow. I'm not sure what we're going to do."

Valentina says, "But Rick loves you, Larisa. And that helps a lot." Again she remembers the old times with Boris. "But no more," she thinks.

— · — · —

Valentina arrives at the Creel Gallery at 8:00 A.M. on Wednesday. Wayne is already there.

Wayne and Valentina go into Wayne's office. He picks up a pile of papers written in Russian. Then he leads Valentina to another, larger office.

"I'm going to put you in Mr. Creel's office, Valentina," Wayne says. "It's the only empty space I have. Please keep the door shut." He hands her the pile of papers. "Translate these notes for me, please," he says; then he hurries off.

THE CREEL GALLERY

Valentina looks around the office. It's a peaceful room, with expensive-looking pictures on the walls. Valentina notices a small Chagall in the corner near the desk. It's a very fine painting.

Valentina pulls her Russian-English dictionary out of her handbag and begins to work. She works steadily, translating half of the pile. Some of the passages are easy; others are very difficult. As a Russian, she knows what the notes are about. She wonders how many Americans will understand the pictures.

One note makes her stop. It's about Socialist Realism. Socialist Realism pictures show happy, laughing workers. They're usually looking at tables full of food. The people in Moscow make jokes about these pictures. "What will Americans think of this?" Valentina wonders. She works on.

At 1:00 P.M. Valentina is hungry. No wonder! Breakfast was a long time ago. She takes out some fruit and cheese from her handbag and eats quickly. Then she returns to her work.

At 5:00 P.M. she finishes and types out her notes. She closes the door of Mr. Creel's office and takes the notes to Wayne.

"Please check my English," she says. "Sometimes my mistakes make the words sound funny."

Wayne looks through the translations and makes a few changes.

"Make sure that the meaning is the same," he says. "Could you please fix the notes so that we can put them near the paintings?"

"Of course," Valentina says. "When do you want them?"

"Tomorrow will do," Wayne says. "Go home now. We have a busy day ahead. The new pictures go up in the afternoon."

After You Read

1. **Write *T* if the statement is true and *F* if it's false. If the statement is false, write the true answer below it.**

    ____ 1. The Creel Gallery belongs to Wayne Briggs.

    ____ 2. Wayne Briggs cannot read Russian.

_____ 3. William Creel had a stroke.

_____ 4. Valentina is an expert on Russian art.

_____ 5. Rick is happy to follow Larisa to Boston.

_____ 6. Valentina works in Mr. Creel's office.

2. **Match the words in column A with their meanings in column B.**

A	B
1. expert	a. likes
2. take care of	b. things that make you laugh
3. is fond of	c. in the future
4. translate	d. parts of a piece of writing
5. passages	e. someone who knows a lot about something
6. jokes	f. look after
7. ahead	g. change from one language to another

3. **Read through Chapter 6 again to find answers to these questions:**
   - What does Wayne Briggs think of Mr. Creel? Does he respect him? Does he like him?
   - Why does Wayne hire Valentina?
   - What is worrying Rick? Why?

4. **Discuss the following questions with your classmates. Make notes on what you decide and report to the rest of the class.**
   - Was Valentina wise to take the job? Why do you think so?
   - What will happen after the exhibition is over?

5. **Do you know anyone who is (or was) seriously sick? What did their friends and family do to help? Tell the class or write about your experience.**

VALENTINA

Chapter 7

The Exhibition

Before You Read

1. **Discuss these questions with your classmates:**
   - What is an exhibition?
   - What do people at a gallery do?
   - What do these phrases mean?
     check off the inventory
     insure the paintings with an insurance company
     pack and unpack the paintings

2. **Look at the pictures on page 46. Greg Foot and Joe Martinez are packing the paintings. Wayne is checking off the inventory. Joe is putting a painting into a crate. Match the numbers on the picture with the words below:**

   _____ painting   _____ crate   _____ lights

   _____ tags   _____ inventory

3. **Think about the pictures and answer these questions:**
   - How do people arrange paintings for an exhibition? What do they need to think about?
   - Is it difficult to exhibit paintings correctly? Why?

The Exhibition

Valentina arrives at the gallery at 8:00 the next morning. The gallery is closed to visitors, but inside everyone is busy.

Wayne is watching two young men take some paintings off the wall. They pack them into special crates. They put the crates into a storage room at the back of the building.

Wayne smiles at Valentina as she enters. She walks over to join him. He has a list with the names of the paintings. He checks each picture off as the men take it down.

One of the men comes over to speak to them. Wayne introduces him.

"Greg, I'd like you to meet Valentina Petrov. Valentina, this is Greg Foot. Greg is Mr. Creel's nephew. He's in charge of installing the pictures."

Greg smiles and looks directly at Valentina. "So you're the one Wayne's hired just for the exhibition," he says. "Glad to meet you." He shakes her hand, then walks away.

Valentina looks at Wayne, who shakes his head. Greg is already back at work.

"That other guy is Joe Martinez," Wayne explains. "He's an artist, a painter. He's hoping to get a scholarship to the Barnes Foundation in Philadelphia. Mr. Creel thinks he will probably get it. He says that Joe is very gifted."

At last the old exhibition is safely packed and stored. Wayne checks the inventory. Every painting is in its place.

It's almost noon. "Take a break, everyone," Wayne says. "The van arrives at 1:00 P.M. with the Russian paintings. Be back here at 10 to 1:00, please."

Valentina eats lunch outside, then hurries back to Mr. Creel's office. She opens the door quietly and is surprised to find Greg Foot there.

"Just thought I'd say hello," he says. He leaves the office quickly.

"He's a strange one," Valentina thinks. But there's no time to worry. She has to retype her notes.

A few minutes later she hears noise outside the office. The Russian paintings have arrived! The men are unloading them from the van. Wayne is watching carefully. Greg and Joe are telling the carriers where to put the pictures. Soon Greg says to Wayne, "They all seem to be here. Do you want to sign?"

"Not yet. I want to check each one," Wayne says. The men wait while he checks the tag of each picture on the list.

Finally, it's time to start unpacking. They move inside. Greg and Joe arrange the paintings. They use Mr. Creel's list. It tells how to group the paintings. They change the lights so that each picture will look its best.

It's a long, slow job.

"What happens now?" Valentina asks.

"Not much more today," Wayne says. "I've checked the inventory for the insurance company."

Valentina looks puzzled. "I don't understand," she says.

"The inventory is the list of paintings. They are very valuable, so they are insured. If somebody steals one, the insurance company will pay. The insurance inspector will come tomorrow to go over the list with me."

Valentina understands now. "We're almost ready to open, aren't we?"

"Yes, but there are still several things to do," Wayne says. "Tomorrow we open at 3:00 P.M. Our party is at 5:00. It's Friday, so I don't expect many people to come before 5:00. They usually come in time for the party.

"Greg and Joe will finish hanging all the paintings tonight. Then tomorrow you'll put the descriptions next to the paintings. I'm going to visit William Creel at 12:30 P.M. After that, the gallery will open."

"I found some books in Mr. Creel's office," Valentina says. "They're about Russian art. May I take them home to read?"

"Of course," Wayne says. "Just be sure to bring them back." He starts locking the back of the gallery. "Oh, one thing, Valentina. A very important art critic will be coming tomorrow. His name is Dr. Peter Malouf. He writes for a big paper. He'll be here at 2:00 P.M., before we open. I'll be showing him around. He can be a very difficult person. If he gives us a bad review, people won't come to the show. And all of this will be for nothing."

"What's a review?" Valentina asks.

"It's an article in a newspaper about an art show. The art critic is the person who writes it. A critic usually knows a lot about the subject."

Valentina nods and says good-bye. She hurries home with the art books. Larisa is out with Rick, so Valentina can sit alone and read.

She sits in a chair with a cup of coffee. Time passes quickly. "I'm just like Boris," she thinks. "Here I am, sitting and reading. And my coffee's cold."

— • — • —

The next day Valentina puts on a special dress for the party. She fixes her hair and makeup with care.

At the gallery, she arranges her notes next to each painting. Then she checks to see that everything is ready. At 12:30 Wayne goes to visit Mr. Creel. Greg and Joe are out for lunch.

Valentina is excited. The exhibition will open soon! She looks around at the pictures. They look wonderful. She is proud to be Russian.

At 1:45, she's still alone in the gallery.

At 2:00 P.M., a man comes to the door.

He introduces himself. "I'm Peter Malouf. Is Wayne Briggs here?" he asks. "He was expecting me at 2:00."

Valentina hears the name "Malouf" and remembers "art critic." What should she do?

"Mr. Briggs isn't here yet," she says. "May I show you around, Dr. Malouf? Or would you prefer to look at the pictures alone?"

After You Read

1. **Write Y (yes), N (no), or M (maybe) before these statements. If you write M, explain your answer to the class.**

    ____ 1. Mr. Creel is Greg Foot's uncle.

    ____ 2. Joe Martinez is an art teacher.

    ____ 3. Greg Foot is very friendly to Valentina.

_____ 4. Wayne will not let Valentina take the art books.

_____ 5. Wayne is late because he had an accident.

_____ 6. Peter Malouf will like the exhibition.

2. **Complete each sentence with one of the words or phrases below:**

checks off	in charge of	install	insurance
review	scholarship	unload	valuable

   1. Wayne looks at the list and _____ the inventory.

   2. Greg is _____ putting up the pictures.

   3. It is Greg's job to _____ the pictures.

   4. A _____ is money to help pay for your education.

   5. Something _____ is worth a lot of money or is very important.

   6. The men take down or _____ the paintings from the van.

   7. If somebody steals the paintings, the _____ company will help pay for them.

   8. A _____ is someone's written opinion or idea about something.

3. **What do you know about Greg? What kind of person is he? Write your ideas on a sheet of paper, then compare answers with a classmate.**

4. **Discuss these questions with your classmates:**
   - Will Peter Malouf give the exhibition a good review?
   - Where is Wayne? How do you think he feels?

5. **Peter Malouf is very important to the gallery. Have you ever had to work with someone important to your job? How did you feel? What happened? Tell the class, or write about your experience.**

VALENTINA

Chapter 8

Peter Malouf's Review

Before You Read

1. **Discuss this question with your classmates:**
   - How does Valentina feel while Dr. Malouf is looking at the paintings?

   Use your own words, or choose words and phrases from this list:

a little scared	angry with Wayne
confident	excited
nervous	proud of the exhibition
tense	worried about Wayne

2. **Look at the picture on page 52. Dr. Malouf is looking at a painting. Valentina is in the background. Match the numbers on the picture with the words below:**

   _____ Dr. Malouf   _____ description

   _____ lights   _____ rain

3. **Think about the picture and answer these questions:**
   - How old is Dr. Malouf?
   - What kind of person is he?

   Use your own words, or choose words from this list:
   cheerful   happy   kind   serious   stern

4. **Look at the picture on page 54. Wayne and Valentina are laughing together. Greg Foot is in the background. Think about the picture and answer these questions:**
   - Why are Wayne and Valentina so happy?
   - How does Greg feel?

Peter Malouf's Review

Peter Malouf steps forward. "I think I'll look by myself first," he says.

"Of course," Valentina replies. She wishes Wayne would arrive soon.

Valentina watches Dr. Malouf as he looks at the paintings. He looks closely at each picture and makes notes.

Valentina finds herself thinking, "Dr. Malouf is quite good-looking. He should smile a little more." His face is very serious. He looks as though it's hard to make him happy.

It starts to rain. Valentina turns on more lights. The pictures look perfect. Joe and Greg have done a fine job.

After a while Dr. Malouf comes back to Valentina. "Can you show me around now?" he asks. "I can't wait around any longer for Wayne Briggs. I have another appointment."

Valentina's heart beats faster. What if she says something wrong? What if Dr. Malouf gives the Creel Gallery a bad review?

"Certainly," she says calmly. They walk slowly around the gallery. Valentina explains how Russian history influenced each picture. Dr. Malouf asks a lot of questions. Valentina answers as best as she can.

"What is your part in this exhibition?" Dr. Malouf demands.

"I translated the notes into English. They were in Russian," Valentina says. "And I'm here because I know about Russia. I love these pictures. They make me proud to be Russian."

After almost an hour, Dr. Malouf is ready to leave. Valentina goes to the door with him. It's still raining quite hard.

Just then, a taxi pulls up outside the gallery. Wayne Briggs steps out, pays the driver, and comes running into the building.

"I'm very sorry I'm late, Peter," he says. "I took the subway to avoid the traffic. Then there was an accident in the subway! We just sat there for more than half an hour. I couldn't get out."

"That's all right," Dr. Malouf says. "I'm going now, anyway. I'll take your taxi before it leaves." He goes before Wayne can say another word.

Wayne looks at Valentina. "What did he say?" he asks. "Was he pleased?"

"I don't know," Valentina says. "I mean, I don't know if he was pleased. He asked a lot of questions."

"Was he angry that I wasn't here?" Wayne asks anxiously.

"I don't think so," Valentina says. "It's very hard to tell." Wayne still looks worried, so Valentina says, "Look at the pictures, Wayne. They look great. Of course he liked them."

But Wayne isn't sure.

A man and a woman enter the gallery. Valentina goes to help them. After a few minutes, they leave.

Valentina spends the rest of the afternoon with customers. Only a few people come.

At 5:00 P.M. the Creel Gallery has its special opening party.

People eat cheese and drink wine. Valentina laughs quietly. Nobody is even looking at the pictures!

After a while people leave the food and look at the art. Valentina listens to what they say. She wants to learn what to tell people. What interests them?

Wayne is talking to the guests. Joe and Greg are mixing with the crowd. Everyone is having a good time.

Suddenly Valentina feels lonely. She looks at a man and a woman standing together in a corner. They look comfortable with each other. "They probably know each other very well," Valentina thinks. The man looks a little like Boris …

"Stop it!" she thinks. "You're here to make a new life, remember?" The man says something to the woman. They both laugh, then leave the gallery. Valentina feels more alone than ever.

"Are you enjoying yourself?" Joe asks. Valentina jumps. For a moment, she forgot where she was. She hopes Joe can't read her unhappy face. She turns to Joe and smiles.

"Some day you'll have an exhibition like this," she says.

"I hope so," Joe replies. "I'm still waiting for a letter from the Barnes Foundation. I want that scholarship so much!"

At 10:00 P.M. the gallery closes. Wayne is depressed. Very few people came to the opening party. Wayne wanted to see more.

"It's a wet night," Valentina says. "People stay inside when it rains."

They lock up and go to their separate homes.

The next morning Valentina arrives at the gallery at 9:00. Wayne greets her with a smile.

"Did you read the paper?" he asks brightly. He pulls her by the arm into Mr. Creel's office. The paper is on the desk.

"Listen to Peter Malouf's column!" Wayne says. He reads: " ' … it's a magnificent exhibition … well chosen' … and then Peter Malouf says this:"

He looks at Valentina to make sure she is listening. "Another plus for this excellent exhibition is Valentina Petrov, a Russian national. Ms. Petrov knows the paintings well. And she knows how Russian history influenced them. The Creel Gallery is showing some great pictures. Ms. Petrov explains them all with knowledge and love." Wayne stops and looks at Valentina.

Valentina doesn't know what to say. She's very excited. Wayne says, "I think we need to celebrate!" They shake hands strongly, then laugh like children. Wayne is still holding the newspaper.

Greg Foot appears at the door. He looks angry.

"No one else's name in the paper, I see," he says spitefully. "Only the translator's." He almost spits the word.

"I think we can say she is more than a translator," Wayne says. "This review will bring a lot of new business. We'll need more help."

He turns toward Valentina. "Are you ready to learn more about sales?"

Valentina smiles at Wayne. "Of course," she says, laughing again. She feels very happy.

After You Read

1. **Number these sentences in the correct order (1–5):**

    _____ Wayne says Valentina can learn about sales.

    _____ Dr. Malouf writes a very good review.

    _____ People come to the opening of the art gallery.

    _____ Valentina shows Dr. Malouf around the gallery.

    _____ Wayne reads the review to Valentina.

2. **Match the words in column A with their meanings in column B.**

A	B
1. magnificent	a. without any fault
2. serious	b. in a very mean manner
3. perfect	c. unhappy
4. influenced	d. excellent; very, very good
5. anxiously	e. in a worried manner
6. depressed	f. changed, made a difference to
7. spitefully	g. unsmiling, not funny

3. **With your classmates, answer the following questions:**
   - How do these people feel about Valentina's new job at the gallery? Why do you think so?

   Larisa: _____

   _____

   _____

   _____

   Wayne: _____

   _____

   _____

   _____

   Greg Foot: _____

   _____

   _____

   _____

4. **With a group, talk about Valentina and the story so far. Look back at Chapters 1–8 and make a graph of the story. Put the happy, positive things at the top. Put the unhappy, negative things at the bottom. Connect the events with lines. Use the chalkboard, or a piece of paper.**

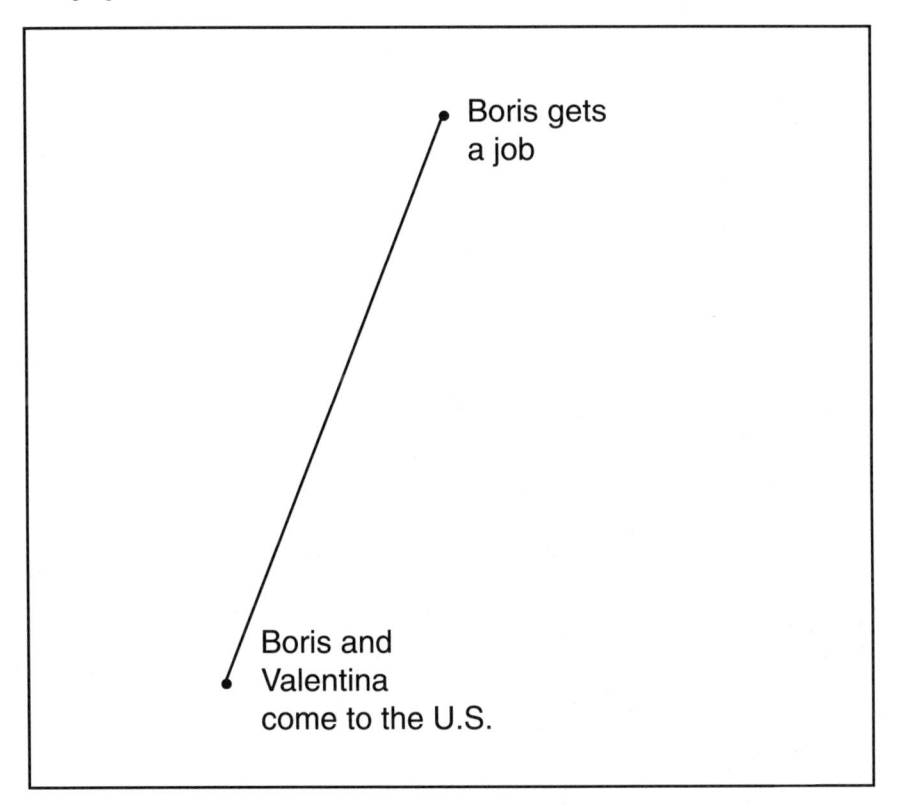

```
• Boris gets
  a job



          /
         /
        /
       /
      /
     /
    /
   /
  • Boris and
    Valentina
    come to the U.S.
```

5. **Imagine you are Valentina. Tell Larisa what happened at the gallery today. Tell her about Wayne, the review, and Greg Foot. Role-play the situation with a classmate. One student can be Valentina, and the other student can be Larisa. OR: Pretend you are Valentina. Write to her mother. Tell her about Wayne, the review, and Greg Foot.**

VALENTINA

Chapter 9

Valentina and Peter

Before You Read

1. **Discuss these questions with your classmates:**
   - Why is the chapter called Valentina and Peter?
   - What do you know about Dr. Peter Malouf?

2. **Look at the picture on page 60. Valentina is saying goodbye to Larisa. Match the numbers on the picture with the words and phrases below:**

   _____ handkerchief   _____ flight information sign

   _____ Rick Oller   _____ airport departure lounge

   _____ suitcase   _____ flowers

3. **Think about the picture and answer these questions:**
   - What do you think is happening?
   - Why is Valentina crying?
   - Where are Rick and Larisa going?

4. **Look at the picture on page 62. Greg is taking down a painting from the wall in Mr. Creel's office.**
   - What is Greg doing with the picture? Why do you think so?

Valentina and Peter

The Creel Gallery is doing very well. A lot of people come to look at the Russian exhibition. And a lot of people buy. Wayne is very pleased with sales.

Valentina works hard. She reads everything she can find about art. Her life at home is very busy, too. Rick and Larisa are getting married. They will go to Boston to live. Valentina will stay in Larisa's apartment. There's a lot to do.

Rick and Larisa are married quietly one Saturday morning. Valentina gives them a little party in the apartment. Then she goes with them to the airport. She cries a little as they say good-bye.

"Boston is very close to New York," Larisa reminds her friend. She passes her a clean handkerchief.

"I know," Valentina sniffs. "But you're such a good friend. I'll miss seeing you."

Valentina returns to the apartment. It seems much bigger now with only one person there.

Peter Malouf often visits Valentina at the gallery. Valentina enjoys Peter's attention. They go to art shows together. They both enjoy the ballet. But Valentina never feels quite comfortable. She was right the first time: Peter Malouf is a very hard person to please.

Valentina's new life is busy. Everything is going well for her.

One morning Wayne says, "Mr. Creel is doing much better.

He'll be able to return to work soon. But first, he wants to meet you. Can you come to his home with me tomorrow afternoon?"

"I'd love to," Valentina says. She wants to meet the man who chose the pictures so well.

At his apartment, Mr. Creel greets Wayne and Valentina from his chair.

"Well, my dear," he says to Valentina, "I think you are doing very well. Wayne tells me you are very good with the customers. You're selling a lot of pictures. Do you want to stay on at the gallery?"

Valentina knows the answer immediately. She smiles and says, "Yes, please."

"Well, we'll talk about it more when I return to work," Mr. Creel says. "My doctor says I can start again next week. Just a few hours a day, at first. We'll see."

They talk for a little while longer. Then Wayne and Valentina leave. They go back to the gallery. Joe is looking after things while they're away.

"A couple came in half an hour ago," Joe says. "They really love one of the paintings. However, they think it's too expensive. They would like you to call them about the price." Joe hands Wayne a business card. Wayne hurries to his office.

Valentina and Joe look at the paintings. They both love working with them.

"There was a phone call for you, Valentina," Joe says. "From Peter Malouf." Joe pauses. "He seems to be calling you a lot lately. Is there something going on between you two?"

Valentina's face gets hot. "I don't know," she replies honestly. "That's the truth. I just don't know." She waits, then decides to say more. "Peter Malouf is a lot like my husband, Boris. They both want to think for me. I'm not sure I want that again. But I do enjoy his company."

She changes the topic. "Speaking of company, Peter's coming to dinner tomorrow night. I must think of something special to cook!"

Greg enters the room quietly and is suddenly standing beside them. "Telephone call for you, Joe. You can take it in Wayne's office. He just went out."

Greg turns to Valentina. "So, the great Peter Malouf is coming to dinner?" he asks sweetly.

Valentina is annoyed. She doesn't want to discuss Peter with Greg.

"Yes," she says, "He is." She walks back to Mr. Creel's office. Greg follows her.

"The gallery owes you something," Greg speaks rapidly. "You bring in a lot of business. Why don't you borrow one of Uncle William's paintings. It would impress Peter. How about the Chagall? He could look at it all night. That would be good for the gallery."

Valentina is interested. She loves the Chagall. She looks at it every day. Peter would enjoy it as much as she does. She knows that.

"I can't do that," she says quickly.

"Of course you can," Greg replies. "It's just like borrowing a book. It's no big deal. Here. I'll get it down for you."

Valentina isn't sure what to do. She feels uncomfortable.

"No," she says. "It's not right."

"Look, I'm the owner's nephew," Greg says. "He's my Uncle William. It's okay, I tell you."

Valentina considers. Should she believe Greg?

A few minutes later Greg is in Mr. Creel's office with a carrying bag. He takes the Chagall painting off the wall and hands it to Valentina. The carrying bag is on the desk.

Just then Joe rushes into the room.

"I got it," he says, "I got the scholarship! I'm going to Philadelphia tomorrow, Friday. I'm going to the Barnes! They want me to spend the day there. I'll see you guys Tuesday when I come back!"

He rushes back out of the room.

Valentina and Greg look at each other, then laugh. It's good to see somebody so happy!

Later that night, Valentina stands in her apartment. The Chagall is hanging on the wall. It looks wonderful. Valentina will start cooking dinner soon.

The telephone rings. It's Peter. "I'm sorry," he says. "I'm calling from the airport. The paper is sending me to Portland, Oregon. I'll be back on Tuesday. Can I come for dinner, then?"

"Of course," Valentina says. She feels a little disappointed as she puts the telephone down. But she doesn't really mind. She can spend the evening with Chagall!

• •

After You Read

1. **Circle the best word to complete each sentence.**

    Larisa and Rick get (1) (*interested   married   annoyed*) one morning. They are going to (2) (*Boston   New York   Portland*) to live. Valentina is (3) (*leaving   returning   staying in*) the apartment.

    Valentina meets (4) (*Mr. Creel   Wayne Briggs   Greg Foot*) at his home. He asks her if she wants to (5) (*look after   go back to   stay on at*) the gallery. Later, Greg finds out that Peter Malouf is coming for (6) (*business   dinner   a party*) at Valentina's. Greg suggests that Valentina (7) (*borrow   buy   cook*) the Chagall to impress Peter.

2. **Circle the phrases (a, b, or c) closest in meaning to the underlined phrases below:**

    1. "Mr. Creel is <u>doing much better</u>."

        a. feeling better

        b. making a lot of money

        c. coming back to work

2. "We'll see."

   a. We'll look at things.

   b. We'll find out what will happen.

   c. We'll have to wait.

3. Joe is looking after things

   a. is taking care of matters

   a. is watching everyone

   c. lost something

4. "The gallery owes you something"

   a. will buy you something

   b. owns a lot of paintings

   c. should repay you in some way

5. "It's no big deal."

   a. It's important.

   b. It's not big.

   c. It's really not important.

6. She doesn't mind.

   a. feels very angry

   b. is pleased

   c. doesn't care

3. Look back at Chapters 1–9. Describe the relationship between Valentina and Greg Foot. Why is he being so nice to Valentina now?

_____

_____

_____

_____

_____

4. **With your classmates, show how people move when they are excited about something. Think of Joe in the story. Now work together to think of words to describe the way excited people move.**

5. **How does Valentina feel when she says good-bye to Larisa? Have you ever felt like that? Tell the class, or write a story.**

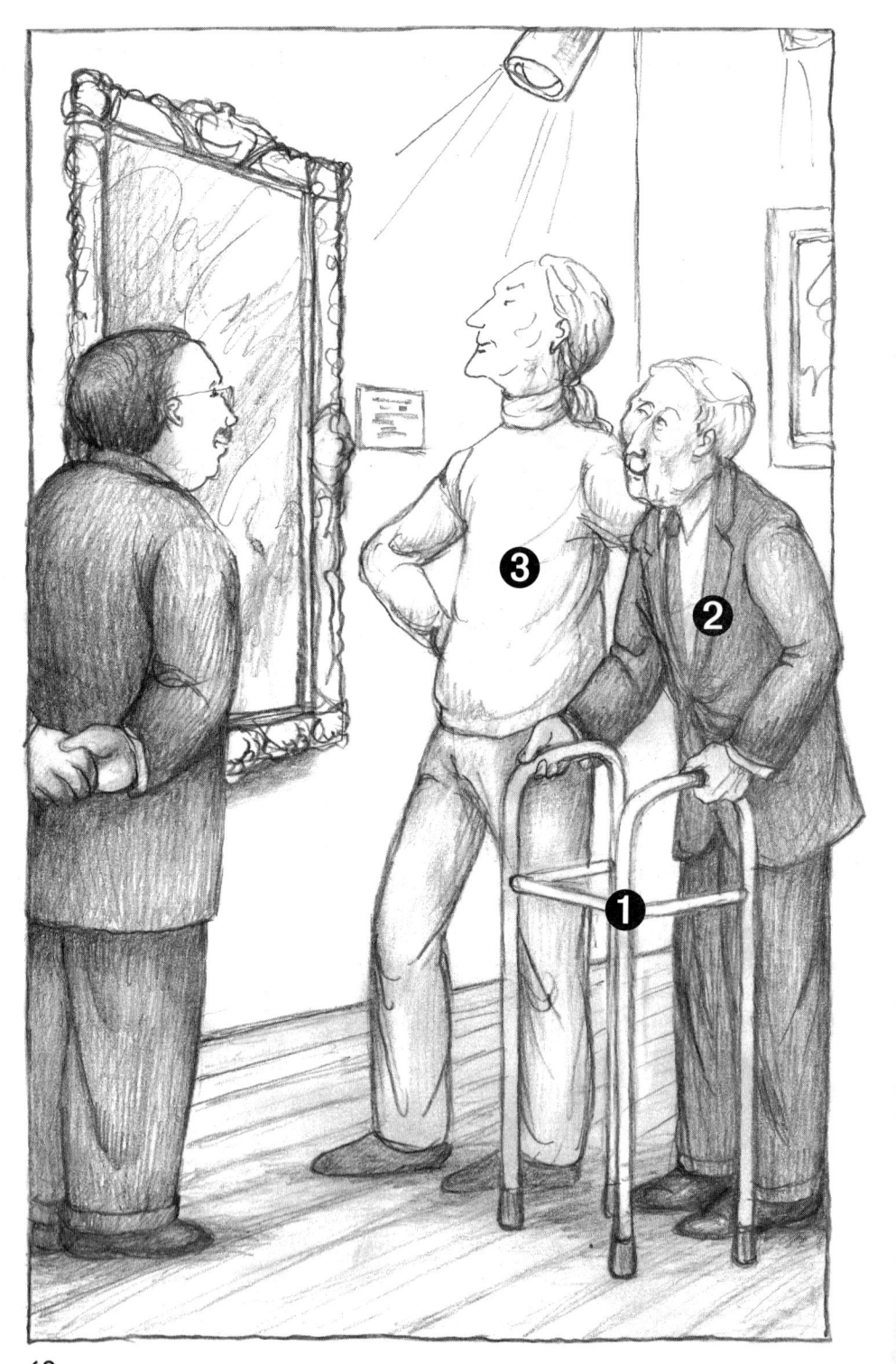

68

VALENTINA

Chapter 10

"Where's My Chagall?"

Before You Read

1. **Discuss these questions with your classmates:**
   - Who is asking, "Where's my Chagall?" Why do you think so?

2. **Look at the picture on page 68. Mr. Creel is leaning on a walking frame. Match the numbers on the picture with the words and phrases below:**

   —— Mr. Creel   —— walker

   —— Greg Foot

3. **Think about the picture and answer this question:**
   - How does Mr. Creel look?

   Use your own words, or choose words and phrases from this list:

angry	exhausted	frightened
furious	guilty	happy
old	proud	sad
scared	sick	still not well
surprised	too tired to move	very upset
very well	weak	

4. **Look at the picture on page 70. Mr. Creel is questioning Valentina. Think about the picture and answer these questions:**
   - How does Valentina feel?
   - How does Mr. Creel look? How do you think he feels?

   Use your own words, or choose words from the list in question 3.

69

"Where's My Chagall?"

Wayne arrives at the gallery at 9:00 A.M. on Tuesday. At noon he hears a familiar voice.

"I'm here to visit," William Creel says. He's leaning on a walker. "Greg drove me over here. The exhibition looks wonderful, Wayne. You've all done a fine job!"

Mr. Creel moves slowly among the paintings. Greg comes to look at them, too. "The lighting is good," William Creel says approvingly, "and the groupings are perfect. You've put the pictures together just right. They're not too close, and they're not too far apart. Nice work, Greg."

"Thank you, Uncle William," Greg says.

The three men look at the paintings. William Creel is very happy, but he's getting tired.

"I'd like to go to my office now, Greg," he says. "I think I'll sit at my desk for a moment."

Wayne and Greg lead Mr. Creel to his office. He sits down and smiles comfortably. "It's so nice to be back," he says. He looks around the room, nodding and smiling.

"Where's my Chagall?" he asks suddenly. "Dear heaven, where's my Chagall?"

Greg coughs. Mr. Creel looks at him. Greg looks away.

"What do you know about this?" Wayne asks.

Greg looks down at his feet. He pretends that he doesn't want to say anything. Mr. Creel's face is red. Wayne is worried. "Speak up, Greg," he says. "Tell us what you know."

"Valentina took it," he says. "You said she could have it, didn't you, Wayne?"

"Of course I didn't!" Wayne says. "When was this?"

"Thursday afternoon," Greg says, "At about 5 o'clock, I think."

"Your aunt gave me that picture, just before she died," Mr. Creel says. "It never leaves this office. Why did Valentina take it? Where is it now?"

"I don't know," Greg says. "Maybe it's at her apartment."

Mr. Creel sinks back in his chair. His face is now pale. He looks very sick. Wayne pats his shoulder. "I'll call Valentina," he says. He picks up the telephone and dials. There's no answer. He checks the number and dials again.

"I'll keep calling," he says. "She's probably out. She has to be here at 2:00 P.M., anyway."

"*If* she comes, that is," Greg says. "The Chagall's a very valuable painting."

Wayne turns and stares at Greg. He is trying to upset Mr. Creel.

Mr. Creel speaks firmly. "I want you to go to that woman's apartment now, Wayne," he says. "Bring her and the Chagall back, too. Now go!"

Wayne looks at Mr. Creel's face. Should he call the doctor? he wonders. Mr. Creel's eyes are angry-looking. Wayne hurries away.

At the entrance to her apartment building, Wayne meets Valentina. She invites him in.

"What's the matter, Wayne?" she asks. "You look upset." They walk into her apartment.

Wayne looks around the room and sees the painting. "I've come to take back the Chagall," he says seriously.

—·—·—

Valentina and Wayne return to the gallery together. They say very little to each other on the way. Valentina knows that she did nothing wrong. But why does she feel like a thief?

At the gallery, Wayne presents Mr. Creel with the Chagall. Mr. Creel holds the painting like a baby. Then he lays it on his desk with care. Wayne goes to stand near the office door to watch for customers.

"Why was this painting in your apartment, Mrs. Petrov?" Mr. Creel asks coldly.

"Peter Malouf was coming to dinner ... " Valentina begins.

"Peter Malouf is in Oregon!" Mr. Creel interrupts. "There's a big art story there. I read about it in the morning paper."

"He called me from the airport," Valentina says.

"Answer my question, please," Mr. Creel says. "Why did you take the Chagall?"

"Greg said that I could take it. He said it would impress Peter Malouf," Valentina says softly. The words sound silly though they're true.

"That's a lie!" Greg says firmly.

Valentina looks at Greg and tries to speak. The words don't come.

"This is very serious," Wayne begins. "You can't just take paintings ... "

"Steal paintings, you mean," Greg corrects.

Valentina suddenly finds the words. "You took the painting

down for me, Greg Foot," she shouts. "You even got a carrying bag for me!"

"That's nonsense!" Greg shouts back. "I didn't touch it. You should call the police, Uncle William. Now."

"Hello!" a cheerful voice calls. It's Joe. He's back from Philadelphia.

"Thank goodness!" Valentina thinks. "Joe will know that I'm telling the truth. But what if he doesn't remember? He was so excited when he left the gallery."

"Joe, do you remember last Thursday? What happened here in this office?" Valentina asks.

"I certainly do remember. That's the day the Barnes Foundation phoned me," Joe says proudly.

"I mean after that," Valentina says hopefully.

"You were very excited," Greg says. "You didn't see anything."

Joe looks at Greg closely. "Well, yes I did, actually." He turns to face Mr. Creel. "When I came into this office," he says, "Greg and Valentina were already here. Greg was handing Valentina the Chagall painting from that wall." He points to the corner of the room.

"I was showing it to her, that's all," Greg says. "What does that prove?" He looks like a child caught lying.

"A carrying bag was on the desk," Joe says.

"Shut up, Joe!" Greg yells furiously. "Nobody ever listens to me. This woman walks in off the street, and everybody loves her. Just once, can't people notice me?" He rushes out of the room.

There's a long silence. Then Mr. Creel says, "I'm sorry about all this. I'd like you to forget it if you can. I'll handle Greg myself. Valentina, I apologize to you. This was a terrible misunderstanding." He leans back in his chair.

Wayne says, "A customer is here. Will you look after her, Valentina?"

Valentina goes into the gallery. She's surprised. When she speaks to the customer, her voice is very steady.

Later that afternoon, Wayne speaks to Valentina. "I had a long talk with Mr. Creel," he says. "We'd like you to stay on as a permanent employee. Will you?"

Valentina looks around the gallery. Despite what happened, she feels happy here.

Valentina smiles at Wayne. "Of course," she says. "This is the new beginning I always wanted."

• •

After You Read

1. **Write *T* if the statement is true and *F* if it's false. If the statement is false, write the true answer below it.**

    _____ 1. Mr. Creel is happy to be back at the gallery.

    _____ 2. Mr. Creel is angry with Greg for the way he hung the paintings.

    _____ 3. Greg does not want to tell Mr. Creel that Valentina has the Chagall.

    _____ 4. Wayne is worried about Mr. Creel.

    _____ 5. Joe cannot remember what happened on Thursday.

2. **These words are from Chapter 10. Choose five of them and write sentences of your own.**

    | excited | furious | glares | impress |
    | police | pretends | showroom | steady |
    | upset | valuable | warning | worried |

    _____

    _____

    _____

_____

_____

_____

_____

_____

_____

_____

3. **With your classmates, show how people's eyes look when they are (a) happy, (b) unhappy, (c) very angry, (d) tired, (e) excited.**

   In the story, Wayne "stares" at Greg. (page 71, line 29). What does "stares" mean?

   Look at the following words. They all have something to do with how people use their eyes:

   blink   gaze   stare

   Show your classmates what each of the words mean.

4. **With your classmates, discuss these questions:**
   - Why did Greg act the way he did?
   - Why is he so angry with Valentina?

5. **Later Wayne speaks to Valentina. "I had a long talk with Mr. Creel," he says. (page 74, lines 1 and 2) What do you think they said? Pretend you are Wayne Briggs and Mr. Creel. With another classmate, role-play their conversation.**